Communism Brainwashing and the Birth of Public Schools

Esther Watchmen

Books by Esther Watchmen

Yoga and Going Green at School:
The Truth Behind the Lies

The Armageddon Movement

Understanding Yoga:
Its Origin and Purpose

Communism, Brainwashing and the
Birth of Public Schools in America

These books are unique because each is a piece
of one massive puzzle that becomes clearer
each time a book is read and reread.

The Birth of Communist Schools in America

America's first education law was passed in 1642. "The Old Deluder Satan Act" clearly documented a profound understanding of the serpent's goal to corrupt the minds of men and devour their souls. The law stated its intent from the beginning: "It being one chief project of that old deluder, satan, to keep men from the knowledge of the Scriptures, as in former time, keeping them in an unknown tongue so in these latter times by persuading from the use of tongues, that so that at least the true sense and meaning of the original might be clouded and corrupted with false glosses of saint-seeming deceivers; and to the end that learning may not be buried in the grave of our forefathers, in church and commonwealth, the Lord assisting our endeavors..."

Four-hundred years ago, there was only one book in many homes: a non-fiction book. Inside its pages lay the most important knowledge of all time from why the stars in the sky represent the days, seasons and years to the revelation of the nature of man. That same book is considered the number one bestseller of all time for good reason. After

4

thousands of years in existence, *not a single sentence contained in that book has ever been proven inaccurate.* Not by scientists. Not by archeologists. Not by anyone - *ever.* Of course, that book was, and is, the Bible. Parents taught their children to read, how to treat others and how to behave appropriately using its powerful words and lessons.

Harvard College was founded in 1636 with the aid of a government grant, as a seminary for educating future magistrates and clergymen. Latin, Greek and Hebrew were required courses because these were the original languages of the Bible. (1)

Among the statues erected at Harvard; are one named "Religion," and another named "Science." The figure representing religion was inscribed, "What doth the Lord require of thee, but to do justly, and to love mercy, and to walk humbly with thy God? Micah 6:8." The statue representing science was inscribed, "The heavens declare the glory of God; and the firmament sheweth His handiwork. Psalms 19:1."

Harvard was established at a time when all schools were strictly local schools, financed locally and controlled locally. There was no central authority just as the colonies and states had no central authority that could wield its power over people in any local area. A Governor and representative legislature existed that exercised a civil authority limited by the higher laws of God. Churches ran the towns, church members ran the legislature and the community lent authority only to those it elected. There was no compulsory attendance law that forced parents to send their children to any state run facility. Private schools flourished because parents preferred them to the charity schools. (2)

Dr. Benjamin Rush, physician, signer of the Declaration of Independence, publisher of the first American chemistry textbook: *A Syllabus of a Course of Lectures on Chemistry*, 1770; co-founder of the First Abolition Society in America; founder of America's first Bible Society that sought to place a Bible in the hands of every graduate; and Treasurer of the U.S. Mint from 1797 to 1813; authored a personal letter in the late 1700's stating his reasons for preferring the Bible as a schoolbook to all other compositions. After much thoughtful consideration, he surmised:

1. That Christianity is the only true and perfect religion; and that in proportion as mankind adopt its principles and obey its precepts they will be wise and happy.
2. That a better knowledge of this religion is to be acquired by reading the Bible than in any other way.
3. That the Bible contains more knowledge necessary to man in his present state than any other book in the world.

4. That knowledge is most durable, and religious instruction most useful, when imparted in early life.
5. That the Bible, when not read in schools, is seldom read in any subsequent period of life. (3)

Dr. Rush wisely observed: "If moral precepts alone could have reformed mankind, the mission of the Son of God into our world would have been unnecessary." (4)

In 1777, *The New-England Primer* was published. This small, lightweight text quickly spread to school-houses across the land. Children began to learn letters by memorizing Bible verses that emphasized morality and good citizenship:

The letter "I" was taught using the sentence, "It is good for me to draw near unto God."

"K" **K**eep thy heart with all diligence, for out of it are the issues of life."

"R" **R**emember thy Creator in the days of thy youth."

"T" **T**rust in God at all times, ye people, pour out your hearts before Him." (5)

Except for the Louisiana Purchase, the War of 1812 and the Battle of New Orleans, quite curiously, not much is ever written or taught about the first fifty years of American history yet, during that time, an event so significant as to set the course of the next 200 plus years took place. This event represented a new kind of war that was quite possibly the most damaging and influential war ever to take place in America. In 1805, Unitarians succeeded in taking over Harvard University and expelling the Christian Calvinists. (6)

These specific Unitarians had a new concept of evil which, they insisted, was not caused by immorality but by ignorance, poverty, social injustice and other environmental issues. It was their assertion that education could eliminate these evils. For them, it was obvious that the creation of earthly institutions would improve the flawed character of man. (7)

1806 brought the Battle of Jena where Napoleon's ragtag amateur army created a military dilemma for Prussia by defeating its professionally trained soldiers. Perplexed Prussian leaders began to search for a solution to their military dilemma. Philosopher Johann Fichte offered the chosen path in his "Address to the German people" wherein he advocated reshaping Prussia's educational system *to prepare students to follow orders given by their government.* (8)

Five main goals of Fichte's plan were intended to shape citizens into: 1) obedient soldiers for the army, 2) subservient civil servants for the government, 3) obedient workers for the mine, 4) subservient clerks for industry, and 5) *to create citizens who thought alike about major issues.* (9)

In 1813 a man in Scotland, Robert Owen, published his "discovery" that man was a product of his upbringing, education and environment, rather than an individual whose character could be formed and trained as the religionists taught. Owen established the Institute for the Formation of Character in New Lanark. (10)

Owen published an essay in 1816 outlining a plan for a national system of education in England that would mold the character of a whole nation which, he asserted, would enhance the good of all. He wrote:

> At present, there are not any individuals in the kingdom who have been trained to instruct the rising generation, as it is for the interest and happiness of all that it should be instructed. The training of those who are to form the future man becomes a consideration of the utmost magnitude for, on due reflection, it will appear that instruction to the young must be, of necessity, the only foundation upon which the superstructure of society can be raised.(11)

In Boston, in 1818, the first move to expand government schools at the expense of private began. This was a complete reversal of the public trend generated by the free people and their free-market forces. In what would later become one of the hallmark techniques for communist activity, adversaries to the private schools began agitating for a state takeover of all schools. The reasons given were that delinquent children were roaming the streets and children of poor families were being deprived of literacy. (12)

A committee was established and a city-wide survey ensued. This survey was the first of its kind ever to be conducted in America. The findings were that 2,360 students attended eight public schools while 4,000 attended nearly 150 private schools. The survey also revealed that 283 children, ages four to seven, and 243 over seven, attended no school at all. This was in spite of the fact that there were no compulsory attendance laws, that most of the schools were private, and that over 90 percent of the city's children attended school. Parents were paying for private instruction and the charity schools were available for those who were unable to pay. *The system was working.* In view of these findings, the committee recommended against state take-over of the schools. (13)

Agitators waged a vigorous campaign in the press never mentioning that more than 90 percent of the city's children were in school. They focused their argument on the nine percent questioning "What are those children doing? Who has charge of them? Where do they live?" They used fear tactics alleging that these children were the targets of abuse who would surely become criminals of the future costing society far more in the long run than the cost of "public" school today.(14)

It was never suggested that the state could subsidize the tuition for any among the nine percent if, in fact, their parents were unable to afford private school and wished to pull their children from the charity schools. This, of course, would have saved the taxpayers an incalculable sum. Instead, the malcontent agitators insisted that all schools become state run facilities where *all* people would pay for *all* children. (15)

1818 was the year Robert Owen, the man in Scotland, proudly presented himself to the world as the founder of the basic principle of moral improvement. Owen is known today as the "Father of Socialism."

The fundamental issues of the nature of God and the nature of man, the foundation stones of our society, began to undergo a progressive change and deterioration.

"Future man" as dreamed by Robert Owen, would later be known as "Soviet man."

From the very beginning, socialists and Unitarians were the prime movers and shakers of the long-range, sustained effort to create government schools. James G. Carter, a Harvard Unitarian, published a series of essays between 1823 and 1825 decrying the trend away from common schools and pushing for expansion of state schools with state-supported teachers' schools.(16)

Robert Owen came to America in 1825. In New Harmony, Indiana, he set up his communist colony. Newspapers generated a great deal of attention to the commune referring to it as "an experiment in social reform through cooperation and rational education." In less than two years, however, Owen's experimental community failed. Rather than accepting the inherent problems with his system, the communist blamed the people raised and educated under the old system claiming they were incapable of adapting to his new model for living. The cult of Owenites decided a national system of secular education would need to precede the creation of a socialist society. (17)

During his opening address at New Harmony, Owen told the gathering:

> I am come to this country to introduce an entire new order of society; to change it from the ignorant selfish system, to an enlightened social system, which shall gradually unite all interests into one and remove all cause for contest between individuals. (18)

Robert Dale Owens, the son of the communist cult leader, together with a man named Frances

Wright, set up headquarters in New York where they organized the Workingmen's Party as a front for Owenite ideas. The cult began giving lectures on socialism and national education and began publishing *The Free Enquirer*, a radical weekly paper filled with antireligious views that turned so many people away from the cult's sad, pagan world-view, they were forced to adopt covert techniques believing the ends would justify the means. (19)

Orestes Brownson, one of the men attracted to the Owenites, was a writer and editor who flipped from Calvinism to Universalism to Socialism to Unitarianism to Catholicism. Describing his brief experience with Owen's cult he wrote:

> "But the more immediate work was to get our system of schools adopted. To this end it was proposed to organize the whole Union secretly, very much on the plan of the Carbonari of Europe, of whom at that time I knew nothing. The members of this secret society were to avail themselves of all the means in their power, each in his own locality, to form public opinion in favor of education by the state at the public expense, and to get such men elected to the legislatures as would be likely to favor our purposes. How far the secret organization extended, I do not know; but I do know that a considerable portion of the State of New York was organized, for I was myself one of

13

the agents for organizing it." (20)

Josiah Holbrook instigated the Lyceum movement in 1829, to organize the teachers of America into a powerful lobby for state education which would become the primary tool for molding children into godless socialists. (21)

From its inception, state education was intended to further the interests of the state. Statist schools were intended to lead to state-ism.

Owenite feminist, Frances Wright, left no doubt that the state would be the ultimate beneficiary of the new, forced, public schools. During a lecture she delivered in 1829, Wright alleged:

> That one measure, by which alone childhood may find sure protection; by which alone youth may be made wise, industrious, moral, and happy; by which alone the citizens of this land may be made, in very deed, free and equal... education; free for all at the expense of all; conducted under the guardianship of the state, at the expense of the state, for the honor, the happiness, the virtue, *the salvation of the state*.(22)

The state is an entity. It doesn't feel happiness. It can't experience salvation. It has no soul. Still this statement demonstrates the purpose and intent of public school: to foster, perpetuate, grow, enhance and protect the state but, to protect it from what or whom? Answer: *the people.*

In 1818, while Robert Owen was declaring his moral superiority to the world, something else was happening in the Prussian city of Trier. A child was born that year to a Dutch immigrant woman and her lawyer husband. 1818 was the year of the birth of Karl Heinrich Marx who would later be hired by the wealthy elites who controlled the "Communist League" to disseminate their goals to the world – without spilling the dirty secret of their ultimate goal: world enslavement for all mankind.

A small group of progressive individuals including Horace Mann of Massachusetts, Barnus Sears of Connecticut and Calvin Stowe of Ohio visited Russia in the early half of the nineteenth century and found everything they dreamed of in a government education system. They found Fichte's plan in action with a few more specificities: state controlled texts with uniform curriculum, full financial support via taxation of the people, forced attendance through compulsory attendance laws, truant officers and teachers trained by the state. *They found the Prussian model.* (23)

Clarence B. Carson in *A Basic History of the United States* explained that government's goal for forced schooling was "...to use the power of the state by way of the schools to *break the hold of religious tradition and inherited culture, and to change society through the child's training."* (24)

Meeting minutes held by Appleton Papers, Massachusetts Historical Society show that on the night of June 9, 1834, a group of prominent men "chiefly engaged in commerce" gathered privately in a Boston drawing room to discuss a scheme of universal schooling. Secretary of this meeting was William Ellery Channing, Horace Mann's own minister as well as an international figure and the leading Unitarian of his day. The location of the meeting house is not entered in the minutes nor are the names of the assembly's participants apart from Channing. Even though the literacy rate in Massachusetts was 98 percent, and in neighboring Connecticut, 99.8 percent, the assembled businessmen agreed the present system of schooling allowed too much to depend upon chance. It encouraged more entrepreneurial exuberance than the social system could bear. (25)

Horace Mann was appointed to fill the position of Secretary of the Board of Education by Governor Edward Everett. Mann immediately began work to create the first "State Normal School" using financial help from prominent Unitarian industrialists, matched by the state legislature which was a state funded and state controlled teachers' college. The school was set up as an experiment in 1838. (26)

Public opposition to Mann's state controlled schools

was strong. The following quote was printed in the *Christian Witness* in 1844:

> We do not need this central, all-absorbing power; it is anti-republican in all its bearings, well-adapted perhaps, to Prussia, and other European despotisms, but not wanted here. (27)

The writer was not referring to the Republican political party. He was referring to *the* republic: America.

Still, in spite of the people, in March 1845, the Massachusetts Legislature appropriated $5,000 in matching funds to the $5,000 raised by Mann's Harvard-Unitarian friends to erect two additional "normal schools." A dedication ceremony was held at one of the schools which Mann described in the *Common School Journal*, October 1, 1846:

> What constituted the crowning circumstance of the whole was, that the Legislature, in making the grant, changed the title or designation of the schools. In all previous reports, laws, and resolves, they had been called 'Normal Schools.' But by the resolves for the erection of the new houses, it was provided that these schools should thereafter be known and designated as *State* Normal Schools, - the State thus giving to them a paternal name, as the sign of adoption, and the pledge of its affection. (28)

As reported in *NEA: Trojan Horse in American Education* by Samuel L. Blumenfeld, James G. Carter made a keen observation in 1825 when he described the linking of state control to teachers' training as a powerful "engine to sway public sentiment, the public morals, and the public religion, *more powerful than any other possession of government.*" (29)

1848 was the year Karl Marx wrote *The Communist Manifesto.* As earlier mentioned, the Communist League hired Marx to package their goals in a nice propaganda style forum for publication and distribution. The *Manifesto* was translated into English in 1850.

As reported by William P. Fall in his 1974 introduction to a reprint of the *Manifesto*, "the (Communist) League itself could be traced back many years, under various names, as a secret and subversive society.

One explicit goal of *The Communist Manifesto* was simply stated for all to understand: *"Free education for all children in public schools."*

Government officials in America would later refer to their controlled schools as "public" while China, after being conquered by Chairman Mao who murdered nearly 50 million people to bring Communism to China, would call his schools "the people's." Both terms have the same psychologically deceptive intent.

Then came Charles Darwin toting the Communist Party line by publishing his theory of evolution *On the Origin of the Species*, in 1851 in an effort to bolster the party's mission to replace divinity with reason (intellectualism/humanism) and religion with nature worship.

It was the following year, in 1852, when America began to isolate her children in government training compounds where, away from their parents, they could be molded into compliant citizens who all thought alike about the major issues of the day.

In 1857, they came for younger children. Kindergartens, developed first in Europe by Friedrich Froebel based on the principle of learning through play (doing), were established beginning in Watertown, New York. (30)

Compulsory attendance was a dream come true for Horace Mann that was echoed by German Philosopher Georg Wilhelm Friedrich Hegel (1770 – 1831). Hegel was considered a philosopher of idealism famous for his professorial speeches in the University of Berlin. Hegel pioneered what is now referred to as the Hegelian Dialect or Dialectical Method whereby an idea (thesis) is challenged by an opposite (anti-thesis) to create a solution (synthesis/consensus) that subsumes both schools of thought. This three part process was perfected by men of ill will to steer and control future events. Desiring to bring about a certain change within society or, implement another control mechanism over the people, cadres of organized men began to create the illusion of a crisis to be used as the thesis followed by the introduction of opposing methods to arrest the crisis and finally, in stage three, to enact legislation presented as a synthesis of consensus or, solution to that crisis. Varying manufactured crises became the topic of the day. Hegelian manipulation of the public quickly became sport among the world's most wealthy men and statesmen.

Consider the two-party system. One presents an idea, the other the opposing idea. From this comes an action or law. In other words, *two opposing forces are created to propel change forward using the Hegelian Dialect.*

Another popular political tool is the Delphi method or, technique, used in government run "community" meetings where *predetermined* "choices" are presented and the public is *guided* into "choosing" a pre-planned outcome. The process is guided by trained "change agents" who, many times, are teachers from surrounding schools or members of various socialist community organizations and planning departments. The "choice" or, outcome, of the meeting is then presented to the larger community as a decision "created by members of the community" when, in fact, shills and peer pressure were used to guide participating dupes into "selecting" a *predetermined* outcome.

Indeed, Karl Marx was an avowed proponent of the Hegelian Dialect incorporating its tenets into his theory of dialectical materialism where two opposing forces – repeatedly, with precise accuracy, under the direction of a "blind force," accidentally, without consciousness, continually struggled over billions of years to produce every exact pattern of life with each reproducing its own kind. Like Darwin, Marx intended to kill off God in the mind's of men and destroy all knowledge of the divine giver of freedom.

Critics worried that Hegelianism (also known as brainwashing) was *"so devoutly godless… that it may call for the destruction of the world"* because it subordinated human beings to the state creating an all powerful government that would devalue the human beings it ruled. (31)

Massachusetts' Census of 1860 revealed tragic results of compulsory state controlled schooling as reported Zachary Montgomery, (nominated as a candidate for U. S. Attorney General) in his book *Poison Drops in the Federal Senate: The School Question from a Parental and Non-Sectarian Standpoint.* Montgomery found that the 1860 census figures showed Massachusetts had one native white criminal for every 649 people, while Virginia, which always left educational control of children to their parents, had only one criminal for every 6,566 residents. In addition, the aggregate figure for suicides in six northeastern states where education was controlled by the state was one to every 13, 285, but in six mid-Atlantic and southern coastal states where parents controlled education, the aggregate figure for suicides was one to every 56,584. Montgomery discovered two reasons for the vast difference. First, the control of children by the state meant the loss of parental authority and home influence and second, state schools neglected moral and religious education and training. (32)

Even so, public schools were established throughout the United States of America and goal number 10 of 10 from Karl Marx's *Communist Manifesto* had been achieved – *almost* as stated:

Free education for all children in public schools.

Free education has cost America more than her people may ever realize - in dollars and *sense.*

In the jargon of psychology, modifying behavior means altering beliefs, attitude is synonymous with viewpoint, and outcomes are the automatic subconscious responses (or world views) a child is supposed to have when he or she leaves school.

B.K. Eakman
Cloning of the American Mind:
Eradicating Morality Through Education

Roots of Communist Brainwashing

In what would later become an all out assault on every mention of God and every symbol of His Being, in every public place across America, the work of malcontent spoilers had already begun on the other side of the Atlantic.

Jean-Jacques Rousseau was among the spoilers. A man of such crooked moral fiber, he gave his own children, five of them, away to strangers and later became a golden-boy heralded by progressive educators. Through repeated actions, he proved his personal fondness for the abandonment of children. Through his writing, he advocated the abandonment of religion as a guiding principle in education.

In 1762, Rousseau published a horrifying book about a young boy that became one of the most influential books ever to come from a twisted human brain. Although it took a quarter century, several Germans became quite intrigued with the images set forth in Rousseau's novel. After Germany, the book spread to America and England where it gained praise from others of like mind. The sickening book was named after its main character, *Emile.*

In this fictional portrayal of a child's training, Rousseau promoted child-centered "permissive education" where the "whole child" should be educated by "doing." (1)

Rousseau's theory was that a "natural education" would free the child from the restraints of custom and tradition. He believed the measure of his programs' success would be determined not by whether it failed to pass on knowledge and skills but, whether or not it produced a citizen fit for the perfect society he envisioned in his treatises.

In *Emile*, Rousseau presented a plan to destroy traditional notions of education and replace them with a theory for creating a new man and a new society. Emile, his title character, was presented as a model. The boy was given a tutor at birth and raised with a "natural education" where he was to learn from "experience." Due to Rousseau's disdain toward any methods of education that inculcated morality, Emile's educational program included no training in the traditional rules of conduct and instead the boy was expected to develop his own rules. Rousseau neglected all usual academic curriculum for Emile demonstrating a good amount of contempt for "heraldry, geography, chronology and language." He believed it was not the teacher's "business to teach (Emile) the various sciences." The teaching method he employed would, whenever possible, be done through "doing" rather than by reading or listening.

Before Rousseau introduces his main character, he gives this portrayal of a nameless student:

> The poor child lets himself be taken away, he turned to look backward with regret, fell silent, and departed, his eyes swollen with tears he dared not shed and his heavy heart with the sigh he dared not exhale.

The student is taken to the schoolmaster. Next comes a reassurance directed toward Emile to inform him that he will never suffer the same fate:

> Oh, you (addressing Emile) who have nothing similar to fear; you, for whom no time of life is a time of constraint or boredom; you, who look forward to the day without disquiet and to the night without impatience – come, my happy and good natured pupil, come and console us. (2)

When one examines the above passages, it becomes clear that the entire scene is couched in negatives. The teacher has put forth no expectation of any positive goals. Instead, he has promised Emile absence of time constraints, absence of boredom, absence of pain, absence of worry, absence of anger or sadness.

Rousseau called Emile's program "negative education." (3)

You see, Emile isn't what one would call "happy."

Nor is he *supposed* to be. He is simply the negative or, opposite of "unhappy." He's *easy*. Yes, Emile, "come and console us."

As New York State *and* New York City Teacher of the Year, John Taylor Gatto, explained in his book *The Underground History of American Education*,

> Emile will learn 'to commit himself to the habit of not contracting any habits.' He will have no passionately held commitments, no outside interests, no enthusiasms, and no significant relationships other than with the tutor. He must void his memory of everything but the immediate moment... He is to feel, not to think. He is to be emptied in preparation for his initiation as a mindless article of nature. (4)

Author Robin Barrow described Emile's tutor as a "detached and manipulative figure" who "guides, controls and manipulates." In reality, the tutor was much more despotic than the usual adult influences in a child's life because his aim was to shape the whole child rather than sharing knowledge and codes of conduct to help the child grow into a thinking, functioning adult. (5)

Rousseau's disciple, Friedrich Gedlike, published the world's first "look say" primer, *A Children's Reader Without the ABC's and Spelling*, in 1791. This text followed the premise outlined by the legendary mystic Comenius in his *Orbis Pictus* from 1657

27

where children were expected to learn using pictures and suggestions. This method was more aptly adapted to the Chinese written language which uses characters rather than phonics as opposed to the English written language composed of letters and sounds. (6)

As reported by John Taylor Gatto, "the average five-year-old can master all of the 70 phonograms in six weeks. At that point he can read fluently just about anything... By the end of the fourth grade, phonics-trained students are at ease with an estimated 24,000 words. Whole-word trained students have memorized about 1,600 words and can easily guess thousands more, but also *unsuccessfully* guess at thousands, too. (7)

Utopian schemes to retard individual maturity in the interest of the "common good" became plentiful after Rousseau's book *Emile.* The ultimate goal was no less than the evolutionary destiny of the species complete with appropriately controlled human breeding which was to be reached through a progressive system of planned change implemented in stages, the first being the orderly scientific management of society where the best people would make decisions unhampered by a free democratic society that benefited from tried and true traditions. The age of maturity was to be delayed and extended to foster *dependence* rather than *independence*.

Just as the terms "with child," and "killing a child in its mother's womb" were given new terms to cloak their true meanings, some time after the Civil War childhood was extended four years and a new word was created to describe very old children: *adolescents.* Old children became a new phenomenon never before seen by the human race anywhere in the world. Oppressive "child" labor laws then began to take shape barring young adults from moving into various fields of productive work. The number of years a "child" was forced to remain in school continued to excel as well as the amount of school required to enter certain "professions." It was all very... *progressive.*

If the earth could "groan" when it "registers another birth" as alleged by Paul Simon in the song "Born at the Right Time," it certainly would have done so when Wilhelm Maximillian Wundt was born in Neckarau, Southern Germany in 1832.

In 1856, Wundt graduated Heidelberg University as a medical doctor. He remained at the school for seventeen years working first as a professor's assistant and later as a professor in the field of psychology. At that time, the term "psychology" meant the study (ology) of the soul (psyche), or mind. (8)

Wundt believed that a thing made sense and should be explored if it was measurable, quantifiable and could be scientifically demonstrated. Knowing no way to do this with the human soul, he advocated that psychology confine itself to the study of experience. (9)

As a result of Wundt's assertion that man was a mere animal, where the mind served as the connection system in a larger stimulus-response mechanism, with no ability for self-determination, he conducted his experiments under the false assumption that a student was nothing more than a body, a brain and a nervous system and education was a process of injecting sensations to manipulate the system. He intended to force the child to produce a predetermined response as a result of certain induced stimuli. Therefore, the actions of a child were thought to be preconditioned precluding the child from choosing his or her individual response to stimuli.

In his thesis, Wundt wrote:

> ...learning is the result of modifiability in the paths of neural connection... The mind is the connection system of man and learning is the process of connecting. The situation-response formula is adequate to cover learning of any sort, and the really influential factors in learning are readiness of the neurons, sequence in time, belongingness, and satisfying consequences. (10)

In other words, controlling the child's experiences

would control the child's thoughts, reactions and therefore behavior leading eventually to a controlled or, "programmed" adult.

While working to inject his radical psyche ideas into the mainstream of German scientism, Wundt redefined psychology as physiological rather than philosophical. In 1875, he established the world's first psych laboratory where he published the journal *Philosophical Studies* as an official organ of this redefined science. (11)

After leaving Heidelberg in 1874 to become a professor of philosophy at Zurich, Wundt subsequently accepted a position in philosophy at the University of Leipzig, in Germany. He was later named rector of the school. He remained at Leipzig for the duration of his career. (12)

Today, many consider Wundt to be the father of experimental psychology. He has been credited for the spread of experimental psychology in the Western hemisphere.

In 1884, five years after Wundt founded his laboratory, Ivan Petrovich Pavlov was in Leipzig studying physiology. It was Wundt's thesis that laid the foundation for Pavlov's hideous experiments which later led American behavioral psychologists to torture people using tactics like electroconvulsive shock treatments and lobotomies. (13)

In his book, *Brainwashing: The Story of Men Who*

Defied It, Edward Hunter relays a haunting experience concerning his viewing of a film used for training purposes by Soviet Russia wherein Pavlov's experiment on dogs *were used on a boy.* Hunter's first attempt to view the film was thwarted because the film he located had been edited to remove its most insidious part. After months of searching, he finally located a copy of the un-cut original. He explained:

> The central theme was indicated by a scene showing a dog in a harness, standing on what looked like an operating table, in a room full of mechanical gadgets and curious meters. What immediately attracted attention was the glass container inserted into the side of the dog's lower jaw. This was supposed to have been painless; it did not seem to annoy the dog. Unsmiling doctors busied themselves with the experiment. One held the bulbous end of a rubber tube. By squeezing it, air pressure moved a circular tray bringing a bowl of food within reach of the harnessed canine. As soon as this happened, a light flashed. The dog hungrily eyed the approaching food, and its saliva began to drip into the test tube attached to its jaw. Each drop was counted and carefully tabulated on a graph.
>
> The dog at first paid no attention to the light. Sometimes the rotary table brought

an empty bowl to the dog's mouth, but whenever that happened, the light did not go on and no saliva flowed. A routine was now established. When the light flashed, food appeared and saliva appeared. When an empty bowl approached, the light did not go on and there was no saliva.

After a while, the dog hardly glanced at the bowl. It had identified the light with the food. The light was sufficient sign; it had 'learned.' The crucial point in the experiment was now reached. A white-gowned doctor pressed a push button, the light flashed, but this time the round table did not bring the dog any food. Its saliva dripped just the same. The light had replaced the food in the mind of the dog, the way a slogan or label can replace a thought in a man's mind. The caption merely read, 'Reflex caused by flashing light.' (14)

Later came the most memorable and most insidious portion of the film which Hunter described as having "the crucial, telltale part" that gave him "a twinge of horror." He knew immediately that this particular portion of the film uncovered "startlingly enough, the message that the communists meant to convey to their hospital interns and to their police practitioners, particularly in the MVD training schools." He wrote:

The incriminating scene began with a young man sitting in a chair, attached to it like the dog in a harness. The switches and push buttons were to operate a combination of gadgets identical to those used for the dog.

A rubber suction tube was stuck into the boy's mouth to measure his saliva. Pills were given him to chew to induce its flow into a glass receptacle. A small cake was waved in front of his eyes, stuck under his nose, and thrust into his mouth. All this was done with grim seriousness. At the same time the light flashed on and off as it had with the animal.

The next scene showed the lad stretched out on a hospital cot like a patient awaiting an appendectomy, except that he was fully dressed. The rubber tube was still inserted into his mouth, its other end projecting into the thin glass receptacle.

A fat cone, with its narrow end open and pointing downwards, was attached to a hinged arm above his head. It was swung over until it hung directly over the boy's face. A push button was pressed by one of the doctors and a few small biscuits were released from the cone into the young man's mouth. Some of these he caught and chewed, others fell down the side of his

face. The light flashed each time the
biscuits were dropped.

The scene shifted again, and the light
flashed without any biscuits falling from the
cone. The boy's saliva flowed just the same.
He was reacting exactly as the dog.

Then Hunter described the experiments' and the
film's evil intent:

This was the part that made the film of such
vital importance to the training laboratories
operated by the Soviet secret police.
Conditioned reflexes could conceivably be
produced to make this youth react like the
dog that rolled over at its trainer's signal.
Only instead of a light, the Kremlin could
use words as signals – any words would do
– imperialism... friend of the people... (15)

Socialist John Dewey joined the faculty of the
Rockefeller-endowed University of Chicago in 1895
where he became the head of the philosophy,
psychology and pedagogy (teaching) departments.
That same year, the university set aside $1,000 to
create a laboratory where Dewey could apply
psychological principles and experimental
techniques to study learning. The Dewey School,
later re-named the University of Chicago Laboratory
School, opened in January, 1896. (16)

Dewey believed the focus of education would have

to shift from the imparting of knowledge and skills to the shaping of children's belief systems and values. There simply was no other way to get them to accept the progressive erosion of freedom he envisioned in the planned march toward complete state control.

An article appearing in *Teacher Magazine* in 1933 revealed much about the damning belief system and values Dewey meant to inject into the nation's children. He wrote:

> There is no God and there is no soul. Hence, there are no needs for the props of traditional religion. With dogma and creed excluded, the immutable truth is also dead and buried. There is no room for fixed, natural laws or moral absolutes.

John Dewey declared that the State should be god, the public schools would be the churches and teachers would be the prophets.

In *My Pedagogic Creed,* Dewey wrote:

> Every teacher should realize the dignity of his calling; that he is a social servant set apart for the maintenance of proper social order and the securing of the right social growth… In this way, the teacher is always a prophet of the true God and the usherer of the true kingdom of God. (17)

As Marlin Maddoux explained in her book, *Public Education Against America*, Dewey was:

> ... an atheist and a socialist who fit the mold of other atheistic social engineers of his time. He was effusive in his praise for Vladimir Lenin in Russia and believed that socialism was the ideal organization for society. Like the communist dictator, he believed that the goals of public education was to bring about 'state consciousness.' He and his socialist friends knew that, in order to get the masses to turn their backs on freedom and embrace socialism, they would have to revolutionize the entire educational system. (18)

Dewey's book, *Psychology,* published in 1896 by the University of Chicago Press quickly became the most widely read and quoted textbook among American educators. (19)

Graduating from Wesleyan University in 1895 was Edward Lee Thorndike, a man trained in the new psychology by the first generation of Wilhelm Wundt's disciples. Thorndike attended graduate school at Harvard where he studied under William James. Here, Thorndike began experimenting with the manipulation of behavior in chickens and pioneered what has come to be termed "animal psychology." Thorndike referred to psychology as the "science of the intellect, character, and behavior of animals, *including man."* (20)

Eventually, Thorndike was accepted to a fellowship at Columbia - a favored recipient of wealth from billionaire George W. Vanderbilt. (21) He packed up his two most intelligent chickens and moved to New York where he expanded his experiments to include other animals including rats and cats. He received a Ph.D. in 1898 and spent the following year teaching at Western Reserve University where he continued his experiments adding mice and monkeys to the mix.

Upon his completion of a visit to Thorndike's classroom at Western Reserve, Dean James Earl Russell, became convinced Thorndike's experiments were worth trying out *on humans.* (22)

Edward Lee Thorndike spent the next 30 years applying his chicken-rats-mice-monkey experimental psychology *on children* at Teachers' College. In 1903, he authored the book *Educational Psychology* asserting that man is an animal that can be studied in a laboratory the same way as mice, fish, cats, chicken and monkeys.

Thorndike extrapolated a set of "laws" from his animal behavior research and applied them to students who intended to become teachers. In turn, these graduates of Teachers' College spread out across the country taking up jobs in every corner of America where they applied the new animal psychology in their classrooms, curricula, schools and students.

In 1908, James Earl Russell, the earlier mentioned Dean of Columbia Teacher's College, appeared as a speaker at the National Education Association's national convention where he made this ominous statement:

> How can a nation endure that deliberately seeks to rouse ambitions and aspirations in the oncoming generations which... cannot possibly be fulfilled? ...How can we justify our practice in schooling the masses in precisely the same manner as we do those who are to be leaders?

Oddly enough, Russell later wrote an article for *Woman's* magazine titled "The Danger of Running a Fool Factory" wherein he pronounced his judgment about the dirty little secret of psych molding. Russell wrote:

> If school cannot be made to drop its *mental development obsession* the whole system should be abolished on the grounds it squanders the resources of the country and wastes the lives of children. (23)

In *The Principles of Teaching Based on Psychology*, 1906, "chicken-man" (Thorndike) provided his definition of the art of teaching:

> ...the art of giving and withholding stimuli

with the result of producing or preventing certain responses. In this definition the term stimulus is used widely for any event which influences a person – for a word spoken to him, a look, a sentence which he reads, the air he breathes, etc., etc. The term response is used for any reaction made by him – a new thought, a feeling of interest, a bodily act, any mental or bodily conditions resulting from the stimulus. The aim of the teacher is to produce desirable and prevent undesirable changes in human beings by producing and preventing certain responses. The means at the disposal of the teacher are the stimuli which can be brought to bear upon the pupil – the teacher's words, gestures, and appearance, the condition and appliances of the school room, the books to be used and objects to be seen, and so on through a long list of the things and events which the teacher can control.

In 1914, Thorndike revealed:

...the progressives in psychology think of man's mind as the organized system of connections or bonds or associations whereby he responds or reacts by this or that thought or feeling or act to each of the millions of situations or circumstances or events that befall him... From this point of

view educational achievement consists, not
in strengthening mystical general powers of
the mind, but in establishing connections,
binding appropriate responses to life's
situations, 'training the pupil to behavior'…
building up a hierarchy of habits…

Following after Thorndike was John B. Watson who
received a Ph.D. from Rockefeller's University of
Chicago in 1903 under the tutelage of John Dewey.
In 1924, Watson wrote:

Behaviorism… holds that the subject matter of
human psychology is the behavior of the
human being.

Watson continued:

Behaviorism claims that consciousness is
neither a definite nor a usable concept.

Meaning these "intellectuals," whose writings are
published by universities, are not convinced they
possess a *conscience*. This consideration may be
what sets them apart from people *with* a conscience
who *know* right from wrong.

Watson wasn't finished. He further declared,

The behaviorist… holds, further, that belief
in the existence of consciousness goes back
to the ancient days of superstition and
magic… The great mass of people even
today… wants to believe in magic… Moses

had his magic: he smote the rock and water gushed out... One example of such a religious concept is that every individual has a *soul* which is separate and distinct from the body... The behaviorist asks: Why don't we make what we can observe the real field of psychology... We can observe behavior – what the organism does or says. And let us point out at once: that saying is doing – that is, behaving...

The rule or measuring rod, which the behaviorist puts in front of him always is: Can I describe this bit of behavior I see in terms of 'stimulus and response'? By stimulus we mean any object in the general environment or any change in the tissues themselves due to the physiological condition of the animal, such as the change we get when we keep an animal from sex activity, when we keep it from feeding, when we keep it from building a nest. By response we mean anything the animal does...

The interest of the behaviorist in man's doings is more than the interest of the spectator – he wants to control man's reactions as physical scientists want to control and manipulate other natural phenomena. It is the business of behavioristic psychology to be able to predict and to control human activity...

> ... how can I, as a behaviorist... get
> individuals to behave differently today from
> the way they acted yesterday? How far can
> we modify behavior by training
> (conditioning)?" (24)

In his book, *Behaviorism*, published in 1925, Watson appealed to parents to surrender their children to the trusted state quietly:

> I am trying to dangle a stimulus in front of
> you which if acted upon will gradually
> change this universe. For the universe will
> change if you bring your children up not in
> the freedom of the libertine, but in
> behavioristic freedom... Will not these
> children in turn with their better ways of
> living and thinking replace us as society, and
> in turn bring up their children in a still more
> scientific way, until the world finally
> becomes a place fit for human habitation? (25)

Watson came to be known as the true father of *behaviorism*.

Dr. W. Horsley Gantt of Johns Hopkins University spent five years of his time in the Soviet Union working in the laboratories of Pavlov on the physiology of the brain. Horsley translated Soviet psychologist Aleksandr R. Luria's book, *The Nature of Human Conflicts*, into English. The book was published in the United States in 1932. The Soviets were experimenting with methods to induce behavioral disorganization in human beings. Luria himself played a major roll in conducting many of those experiments.(26)

Gantt set up the Pavlovian Laboratory in the Phipps Psychiatric Clinic of Johns Hopkins University in 1930. Additionally, he established the Pavlovian Society for Research and served as editor-in-chief of the *Pavlovian Journal of Biological Psychiatry*. These activities help to demonstrate an *intimate relationship between Soviet and American psychiatry and psychology.* (27)

In the book Gantt translated, Luria wrote:

> The researches described here are the results of the experimental psychological investigations carried on at the State Institute of Experimental Psychology, Moscow, during the period of 1923 – 1930. The chief problems of the author were an objective and materialistic description of the mechanisms lying at the basis of the disorganization of human behavior and an experimental approach to the laws of its regulation... To accomplish this it was necessary to create artificially affects and models of experimental neuroses which made possible an analysis of the laws lying at the basis of the disintegration of

behavior. (28)

In the first chapter of his book, Luria wrote:

> Pavlov obtained very definitive affective
> 'breaks,' an acute disorganization of
> behavior, each time that the conditioned
> reflexes collided, when the animal was
> unable to react to two mutually exclusive
> tendencies, or was incapable of adequately
> responding to any imperative problem. (29)

"Breaks" were induced with the "look-say" method
and subsequently "diagnosed" as dyslexia. Rather
than teach the alphabet and phonics, children were
taught words using pictures as is done with Chinese
symbols. Prior to 1930, there were almost no cases
of dyslexia yet, today in America, it is the most often
diagnosed learning disability. *Which is the reason
"look-say" is not used in communist Russia!*

"Behaviorists" B.F. Skinner and Alfred C. Kinsey, two
of the most morally bankrupt individuals ever to
enter the teaching profession, (or any other)
published their books, *Walden Two* and *Sexual
Behavior in the Human Male* in 1948. Skinner's
novel, *Walden Two,* argued his desire to have
children "reared by the state, to be trained from
birth to demonstrate only desirable characteristics
and behavior." Kinsey pried sexuality from the
confines of love and marriage in pursuit of the
grand scheme to move America and the world
toward the eugenic future envisioned by elite

planners. This latter shift caused a domino affect felt throughout educational, legal and medical professions. Not to mention the damning affects on family life and the rights of the unborn child. Getting through the incubation period in the safest place a child will ever rest, its mother's womb, would become one of the most dangerous places for the tiniest humans. Unborn animals and birds would later possess more rights than the unborn child thanks to humanist, activist judges who discarded all previous case law to create new legal precedents. (30)

Skinner is another education guru who is widely exalted by the establishment yet, once again, a dark secret about the man lurks throughout his character. B.F. Skinner, heralded as the most famous behaviorist from Harvard, could realistically be described as a terrorist. Skinner raised his own daughter in a sealed container with signaling levers and a food chute called the "Skinner Box" or, more appropriately titled, a psychological torture chamber. While B.F.S. struggled to learn something unrealistic about child behavior in captivity, it is another gross fraud to link any measurement of success to his amoral, criminal behavior. Skinner's daughter killed herself when she was 21. (31)

In his book, *Walden Two*, Skinner portrayed a utopian society achieved through behavioral engineering, run by a totalitarian dictator. Like in the book and movie, *The Giver*, every citizen was placed in a sterile cubicle for his first year of life where his psychological conditioning began. The end of the book is reminiscent of the movie "The Truman Show" where the puppet-master is seen struggling to maintain control. As Negley and Patrick explained in *The Quest for Utopia,* the perp who built what he believed to be the perfect little town peers down from a nearby hill overlooking the brainwashed, docile community he created and proclaims: "I like to play God!"

This may be the reason the Vanderbilt funded Grand Central Terminal in New York has an enormous astrological mural on the ceiling with the stars painted *backward* over the heads of 750,000 daily commuters. They are backward as if one is looking *down* on the people from the *other* side: as if the onlooker is god.

Treating pupils as guinea pigs was Skinner's norm. He once revealed, "We can achieve a sort of control under which the controlled nevertheless feel free, though they are following a code much more scrupulously than was ever the case under the old system." (32)

Tragically, the education establishment was so enamored with B.F. Skinner, he was propelled onto the speaker circuit where he promoted his secrets of mass behavior manipulation to business execs and earned a hefty sum.

Skinner wrote a number of books throughout his

career. In 1953, he published another significant thriller titled: *Science and Human Behavior.* Consider this startling excerpt:

> … we may "blame" someone for an unfortunate event which was not actually the result of his behavior, although the temporal relation was such that a contingency can be asserted. "If you hadn't dawdled so, we should have started earlier, and the accident never would have happened." We blame him in order to alter his future behavior – to make him less likely to dawdle, and we achieve this by converting an unrelated event into an effective punishing consequence through certain verbal processes. (Lying) We use the event as a punishment, even though we did not actually arrange the contingency. (The "accident.") It is only a short step to claiming the ability to arrange such contingencies. *This is the underlying principle of witchcraft.* Unless the controlee behaves according to command, the controller will bring bad luck to him. The threat to do so may be as powerful as the infliction of comparable physical punishment. (Emphasis added) (33)

Skinner documented the fact that children are being "trained' and "conditioned" *using the principles of witchcraft!*

In 1949 the University of Chicago Press published *Basic Principles of Curriculum and Instruction* by Professor Ralph Tyler, chairman of the Department of Education at the University of Chicago (later appointed as the Carnegie Corporation's Chairman of the Committee on Assessing the Progress of Education which stated:

> Since the real purpose of education is not to have the instructor perform certain activities but to bring about significant changes in the student's pattern of behavior, it becomes important to recognize that any statement of the objective... should be a statement of changes to take place in the student. (34)

Impact of Science upon Society, Columbia University Press, 1951, by Bertrand Russell, calls attention to the behavior modification techniques used on students causing them to question and ultimately reject traditional values and to submit willingly to totalitarian controls:

> Education should aim at destroying free will so that after pupils are thus schooled they will be incapable throughout the rest of their lives of thinking, or acting otherwise than as their school masters would have wished... Influences of the home are obstructive; and in order to condition students, verses set to music and

repeatedly intoned are very effective... It is
for a future scientist to make these maxims
precise and discover exactly how much it
costs per head to make children believe that
snow is black. When the technique has
been perfected, every government that has
been in charge of education for more than
one generation will be able to control its
subjects securely without the need of
armies or policemen. (35)

In 1953, Professor Benjamin Bloom, with help from
Professor David Krathwohl, completed *Taxonomy of
Educational Objectives* – explaining the principles of
scientifically classifying cognitive, affective and
psychomotor "domains" of learning. "Scientific
classification" relating to education of a human
being involves breaking behavior down into
categories to be measured and observed which can
then be isolated from the human personality with
its spiritual dimension.

In *Taxonomy,* which later became known as the
"Educator's Bible," Bloom stated that:

> ...the philosopher, as well as the behavioral
> scientist must find ways of determining
> what changes (values) are desirable and
> perhaps what changes are necessary.

He opined that a schools' attempt to alter its
students' values was a virtual "Pandora's Box," but...

> Our "box" must be opened if we are to face reality and take action, and that it is in this 'box' that the most influential controls are to be found. The affective domain contains the forces that determine the nature of an individual's life and ultimately the life of an entire people. (36)

Bloom and Alfred Kinsey were involved in the breaking apart of man (taxonomizing) into what they referred to as units of behavior. This breaking down was the act of scientifically deconstructing man which was intended to separate man from his God-given, individual worth and identity. Such focused efforts were expected to aid in developing methods to control man and society.

Benjamin Bloom helped to create Outcome Based Education curriculum based on Skinner's operant conditioning system.

By 1953, behavioral psychology had completely revised *all* classroom curriculum in America.

The January, 1962 publication of the *Journal* displayed an article titled "The Teacher – Agent of Change" revealing how social psychology was being applied in the classroom. It contained these statements:

> National Training Laboratories of NEA initiated a program for classroom teachers... The training lab is an intensive learning

experience... in which a staff of social scientists help translate research findings into classroom practice. Objectives include greater sensitivity in observing and interpreting social and psychological factors in learning groups... (37)

The National Training Laboratory (NTL) was created in 1947. Its first laboratory session on group processes and human relations was conducted at Gould Academy in Bethel, Maine. The lab's founders had truly relevant connections with the Office of Strategic Services (OSS) which was the forerunner to the Central Intelligence Agency. NTL together with the NEA became the premier change agent/brainwashing agency. (38)

In fact, a book published jointly by these two agencies in 1962 titled *Five Issues in Training* addressed the process of *"unfreezing, changing, and refreezing" attitudes* to bring about change stating:

The Chinese communists would remove the target person from those situations and social relationships which tended to confirm and reinforce the validity of the old attitudes. (39)

This radically disturbing process is now widely used in education, theology, medicine, business, government, etc., by pressuring people to participate in "retreats," that remove them from familiar surroundings to "unfreeze" their attitudes and values. Bethel, Maine's NTL has hosted people from all over the world. Consider this excerpt from a 1977 issue of *NTL Newsletter:*

> From the New Britain workshop dialogues of the founders emerged the notions of "action research laboratory" and "change agent" which were terms coined to denote a very vigorous proactive social change kind of posture, a merging of radical education, deviant behavioral science, and humanistic democracy.(40)

Mental Robots by Dr. Lewis Albert Alesen was published in 1953. Alesen also authored *The Physician's Responsibility as a Leader.* Excerpts from *Mental Robots* taken from chapter seven titled "The Tools of Robotry" follow:

> Herbert A. Philbrick (double agent and author of *I Led Three Lives*) has been recently quoted as stressing that Soviet psychiatry is the psychiatry of Pavlov, upon whose original work on dogs (and boys) the theory of the conditioned reflex is based. This conditioned reflex is the principle underlying all of the procedures employed by the Soviets in their brain-washing and brain-changing techniques. Under its skillfull use the human can be, and has been in countless instances, so altered as completely to transform the concepts previously held and to prepare the individual

so treated for a docile acceptance of all manner of authoritarian controls. The psychiatrist boasts that he possesses the power to alter human personality, and he has certainly made good his boast in many respects, at least to the extent of being able to force phony confessions out of men like Cardinal Mindszenty, Robert Vogeler, and a host of others who have been subjected to all manner of torture during their period of conditioning. (41)

In a book entitled *Conditioned Reflex Therapy* by Andrew Salte, published in 1949 by the Creative Age Press, individual free will, freedom of choice, and, of course, individual responsibility are categorically denied in these words:

We are meat in which habits have taken up residence. We are a result of the way other people have acted to us. We are the reactions. Having conditioned reflexes means carrying about pieces of past realities… We think with our habits, and our emotional training determines our thinking. Where there is a conditioned reflex, there is no will. Our 'will power' is dependent on our previously learned reflexes.

Certainly it is true that the Communists, both in Russia, China, and the Iron Curtain countries, have accomplished spectacular changes in the thinking of millions of their citizens. Whether or not this mass changing is altogether sincere or durable is not for the moment as significant as the fact that it has taken place, and that based upon it there has been, apparently, a ready acceptance of revolutionary doctrines radically defying former custom and accepted usage, and transforming the individual under this spell of persuasion or compulsion into an individual possessing entirely different characteristics from those formerly exhibited. And thus, whole new social, economic, political, and even religious regimes have been accepted in comparatively short time.

In order to comprehend at all adequately what has been and what is happening to the mental processes and attitudes of the American people during recent years, and in order most particularly to be aware of and alert to the carefully planned goals of the inner and hard-core sponsors of the so-called mental health program, it is pertinent to explore briefly the science and art of cybernetics. Cybernetics, according to Gould's medical dictionary, 'The science dealing with communication and communication-control theory as applied to mechanical devices and animals; and including the study of servo-mechanisms, that is, feed-back mechanisms; Josiah Macy, Jr. Foundation,

565 Park Avenue, N.Y. 21, N.Y., has published a series of symposia on cybernetics "Circular Causal and Feed-Back Mechanisms in Biology and Social Systems." (42)

In a Freedom Forum presentation entitled "Inside U.S. Communism" by Herbert Philbrick, at Harding College, Searcy, Arkansas, April 16, 1954, and distributed by the National Education Program, Mr. Philbrick had this to say about cybernetics:

> The Communists, I have discovered, have a favorite term for their system of influencing people in devious ways. The word they use as an over-all title of this technique is 'cybernetics.' Cybernetics as a pure science has a very legitimate and worth-while function. It has to do with how to improve conduits and cables, how to make better coaxial cables for television, how to improve telephone service, how to make more efficient electronic brains, etc. It has a very legitimate service as pure science.
>
> But since a human being, to a Communist, is simply another machine; since human nerve centers have exactly the same function as an electronic circuit; since a human has not a soul – he is only a mechanical apparatus – the Communists have decided that this particular science has a very useful application – not on machines but on humans.

Now we've heard a great deal more recently about brain-washing. Back in 1940 that word wasn't familiar to us, but what was going on inside these Young Communist League cells was a technique of cybernetics, a technique of brain-washing, if you will; the highly developed science of *demolishing the minds and the spirits of men.* (emphasis in original) … The Communists have decided that cybernetics provides a very wonderful way to go to work on healthy minds and to destroy them. And of course we are now getting a bit of that picture from our own prisoners of war who were jailed and imprisoned by the North Koreans and the Red Chinese… It's a horrifying story.

…It is based on the findings of Pavlov which say that a man, like an animal, conditioned to respond to certain impulses, can be conditioned to respond to words, phrases and symbols… It is the scientific control of human beings by means of control (of) information. (43)

Carol Denton authored an article titled "People Control Blueprint" which was published in the May, 1972 issue, Vol. 3, No. 12, of *The National Educator* that echoed the April 6, 1971 Michigan Governor's Advisory Council on Population paper. The "Blueprint" stated:

> A "Top Secret" paper from the Center for the Study of Democratic Institutions, now in

the hands of *The National Educator*, reveals a plan for total control of the people of the United States through behavioral modification techniques of B.F. Skinner, the controversial behaviorist author of *Beyond Freedom and Dignity*...

According to the "Dialogue Discussion Paper," marked "Top Secret" across the bottom of the cover page, a conference was held at the Center on January 17 through 19, 1972,at which time a discussion on 'The Social and Philosophical Implications of Behavior Modification' was held. The paper in question is the one prepared (by) four individuals for presentation at that conference entitled, 'Controlled Environment for Social Change.' The authors are Vitali Rozynko, Kenneth Swift, Josephine Swift and Larney J. Boggs...

... Page 3 of the paper states that the 'Top Secret' document was prepared on December 31, 1971...

The authors of this tome are senior staff members of the Operant Behavior Modification Project located at Mendocino State Hospital in California and the project is partially supported by a grant from the National Institute on Alcohol Abuse...

On page 5 of this blueprint for

totalitarianism, the authors state that "we are presently concerned with controlling upheavals and anarchic behavior associated with social change and discontent..." The authors go on to say that they believe an "Orwellian world" is more likely under presently developing society than under the kind of rigorous controls of a society envisioned by Skinner...

On page 6, the authors deplore the growing demands for "law and order," stating that the population is now more apt to support governmental repression than previously, in response to "their own fears"...

They add that "with the rising population, depletion of natural resources, and the increase in pollution, repressive measures may have to be used to guarantee survival of our species. These measures may take the form of forced sterilization, greatly restricted uses of energy and limits on population movement and living location...

Skinner, on the other hand, they allege – "advocates more sophisticated controls over the population, since punishment (by the government) for the most part works only temporarily...

On the other hand, the authors allege, operant conditioning (sensitivity training)

and other behavioral techniques can be
used to control the population through
'positive reinforcement.' (44)

All Our Children Learning by Professor Benjamin
Bloom was published in 1981. On page 180, Bloom
stated:

> The purpose of education and the schools is
> to change the thoughts, feelings and actions
> of students.

Further, Bloom wrote on pages 33-35:

> (T)he International Association for the
> Evaluation of Educational Achievement
> (IAEEA) is an organization of 22 national
> research centers which are engaged in the
> study of education... This group has been
> concerned with the use of international
> tests, questionnaires, and other methods to
> relate student achievement and attitudes to
> instruction, social and economic factors in
> each nation. The evaluation instruments
> also represent an international consensus
> on the knowledge and objectives most
> worth learning. (45)

A letter to the editor printed on the *Washington
Post's* editorial page by Donald K. Pumroy,
University of Maryland professor of Education and
Psychology and the director of the university's
 psychology program on June 16, 1990 stated:

> It is the teacher's job to change the behavior of his or her pupils. The theory and technique are based on research that goes back several decades, and we know they work because of this research. While many individuals do not understand or appreciate the behavioral position, there are serious efforts underway to help teachers learn and use this approach in their classes. The general public will hear more of the science of behavior in the future.(46)

In 1995, Ronald G. Havelock came out with his second edition of *The Change Agent's Guide*. In his acknowledgments he wrote:

> The original development work which led to the first edition of The guide was supported under contract with the United States Office of Education in the late 1960's and early 1970's. Special credit for sustained encouragement and support belonged to the late Thomas C. Clemens of the U. S. Office of Education... Thanks also goes to the 115 educators across the United States who reviewed the first draft of The Guide and provided helpful comments. At the time of the original publication, the senior author was Program Director and Research Scientist at the Institute for Social Research, University of Michigan, Ann Arbor... The

return of 'change' as a buzzword in education and other fields has prompted the extensive revision and reissuance of The Guide... It is now offered to a new generation of change agents who are making their way in the reform environment of the 1990's.

In The *Guide's* foreword Matthew B. Miles stated:

What do we know about how to support and encourage change?

...The truth is that not until the late 1940's, when American behavioral scientists began exploring and developing the ideas of the émigré psychologist Kurt Lewin, did we really have anything like a systematic science and practical craft of planned change in the kinds of social systems that matter most – families, small groups, organizations, communities.

Meaning they want to impose themselves on *your* family and everyone in *your* community because, after all, *they* know best what is good for *you* and *your children.*

Miles continued:

... Ron Havelock's classic research which resulted in the first edition of this book brought together 3,931 studies on how planned change proceeds most effectively.

In Part Two: The Stages of Planned Change, Havelock and his co-author draw on a three stage brainwashing model invented by Kurt Lewin known as "Unfreeze – Move – Refreeze." This three part system is often employed under different titles such as "Storm – Form – Re-norm." The first time this author became aware of this *illegal* mind-altering system was when high school students were chosen by their teachers to attend a three day re-education event called "Camp Mini-Town" which was conducted by the National Center for Community and Justice formerly known as the National Conference for Christians and Jews obviously eliminating the need to change their moniker: NCCJ. Other names for Camp Mini-Town were Camp Any-Town, Camp Metro-Town and Camp Uni-Town.

The deception of Camp Mini-Town ran deep. Students were told they were "chosen" making them feel like they were "special." Parents were allowed to attend an introduction speech while their children were taken to another area. Parents were not told that the entire focus of the "camp" was to tear asunder all moral absolutes and replace them with relativism based on feelings. Students were kept up late and forced to rise early. Activities filled the days. When they arrived back at their homes, their minds were still busy processing the newly "frozen" situational ethics based on the empty philosophy of humanism.

Proudly parading themselves to the next school board meeting dressed in gray (gray being the mix of black and white "absolutes" meaning everything is "gray and nebulous") students were clothed in T-shirts advertising the name of the camp. As their change agents wished, they shouted their intent to set up a homosexual group in one of the classrooms. In the morning they passed out literature promoting a "Day of Silence" for gays, lesbians, bisexuals and trans-genders (LGBT). The "community organizers" behind the campaign along with school administrators and teachers who had previous knowledge of the "change" to be orchestrated, anxiously obliged with the pre-arranged requests while allowing the chosen students to think it was their own idea.

In 1960, *Teaching Machines and Programmed Learning: A Source Book* was published by the Department of Audio-Visual Instruction, National Education Association, Washington D.C. The book was edited by A.A. Lumsdaine, program director of the American Institute for Research and professor of education at University of California Los Angeles; and Robert Glaser, professor of psychology at University of Pittsburgh and research advisor at the American Institute for Research. Following are a few excerpts:

> *The Science of Learning and the Art of Teaching*
> by B.F. Skinner

Recent improvements in the conditions which control behavior in the field of learning are of two principal sorts. The 'law of effect' has been taken seriously; we have made sure that effects *do* occur and that they occur under conditions which are optimal for producing the changes called learning. Once we have arranged the particular type of consequence called a reinforcement, our techniques permit us to shape the behavior of an organism almost at will. It has become a routine exercise to demonstrate this in classes in elementary psychology by conditioning such an organism as a pigeon.

In all this work, the species of the organism has made surprisingly little difference. It is true that the organisms studied have all been vertebrates, but they still cover a wide range. Comparable results have been obtained with rats, pigeons, dogs, monkeys, human children, and most recently – by the author in collaboration with Ogden R. Lindsley – with human psychotic subjects. In spite of great phylogenetic differences, all these organisms show amazingly similar properties of the learning process. It should be emphasized that this has been achieved by analyzing the effects of reinforcement and by designing techniques which manipulate reinforcement with considerable precision. Only in this way can the behavior of the individual organism be brought under such precise control. It is also important to note that through a gradual advance to complex interrelations among responses, the same degree of rigor is being extended to behavior which would usually be assigned to such fields as perception, thinking, and personality dynamics." (47)

Wendt, Thorndike, Pavlov, Watson, Marx, Darwin, Freud, Beria, Skinner, Bloom, Havelock, Lewin and their sinister cohorts were all perfectly aligned with Soviet Russia and the plan to wrest the consciousness and souls of men from the God of creation and hurl them all in the opposite direction.

Professor E. Merrill Root of Earlham College published his book, *Brainwashing in High Schools,* in 1958. Inside the pages, Root shared the views of army psychiatrist and brainwashing expert Major William E. Mayer quoted in *U.S. News & World Report* as stated on February 24, 1956. Major Mayer related an example of successful brainwashing of about one-third of the American prisoners of war under North Korean Communists. The Major indicated that the formal education received in America failed to provide the men with historical knowledge of our country that would have aided the troops to counter the Communist brainwashing techniques. When the reporter asked, "Weren't they taught this (knowledge of the American system) in school?" Major Mayer responded, "Many of them said they didn't know."

Root also cited a report by the Defense Department
Advisory Commission on Prisoners of War issued by
Joint Chiefs of Staff chairman Admiral Arthur
Radford dated July 29, 1955 that reached similar
conclusions. Professor Root explained:

> Politically speaking, our government is not a
> 'democracy' but a constitutional republic,
> with checks and balances designed to curb
> the public state and to enhance the
> individual. (48)

March 13 of that same year, 1958, Edward Hunter,
who worked for numerous American and foreign
newspapers, testified in front of Congress:

> These (subtle brainwashing) developments
> include the penetration of our leadership
> circles by a softening up and creating a
> defeatist state of mind. This includes
> penetration of our educational circles by a
> similar state of mind... the liquidation of our
> attitudes on what we used to recognize as
> right and wrong, what we used to accept as
> absolute moral standards... by dialectical
> materialism... The objective of all
> communist conquest is simply use for
> power. They seek to conquer the United
> States in a manner so that it "voluntarily"
> falls into the Red (communist) orbit. If we
> have to be conquered by destructive

nuclear-age weapons, it will be considered a setback by the Kremlin. Their objective is to make the same use of the American people as they make of the Czechs in the uranium mines of Czechoslovakia, and as they make of the Chinese in the mills of China. We are to become subjects of a "New World Order" for the benefit of a mad little knot of despots in the Kremlin. (49)

Per the Congressional Record for October 10, 1962, Representative John Ashbrook stated that his intent when introducing House Resolution 10508 was to curb abuses in testing programs in schools. He reported that Health Education and Welfare counselors in our schools were asking questions such as, "Is it wrong to deny the existence of God?" He noted Emily Cuyler Hammond's intensive study of testers in Germany during the 1930s "using the Freudian art of motivation research to reach and manipulate young minds." Ashbrook warned that the United Nations Education, Scientific, Cultural Organization's opinion of "right attitudes" could

...lead our youth down the path to collectivism and internationalism whereby they gradually lose their loyalty to home and nation... their first loyalty will be to world government. (50)

Ashbrook said the former Director-General of the World Health Organization and 1959 Humanist of the Year, Dr. Brock Chisholm, hopes re-education, free from moralities, will lead to "a new world" that "can be molded and children prepared for world citizenship." He said Chisholm advocated "our close watch on each other and everyone in the world should not be relaxed for a moment." And he drew attention to HEW's "Project Talent" from 1960 that planned "to check up for the next 20 years on the personality scores of those who took the exams." He also described HEW's 1961 report titled, "A Federal Education Agency for the Future," as a "blueprint for making American education Federal rather than local in nature." Ashbrook quoted the author of a confidential report to the Office of Education Committee on a Federal Education Agency for the Future saying it disclosed "the deliberate and planned effort to influence on an extensive, nationwide scale, thinking in American education." (51)

On February 1, 1993, *Forbes* published *"Indoctrinating the Children"* by Thomas Sowell. Dr. Sowell wrote:

> The techniques of brainwashing developed in totalitarian countries are routinely used in psychological conditioning programs imposed on American school children. These include emotional shock, desensitization, psychological isolation from sources of support, stripping away defenses, manipulative cross-examination

of the individual's underlying moral values by psychological rather than rational means. These techniques are not confined to separate courses or programs.   Are not isolated idiosyncrasies of particular teachers. They are products of numerous books and other "educational" material in programs packaged by organizations that sell such curricula to administrators and teach the techniques to teachers. Some packages even include instructions on how to deal with parents or others who object... Stripping away psychological defenses can be done through assignments to keep diaries to be discussed in the group and through role-playing assignments, both techniques used in the original brainwashing programs in China under Mao. (52)

The February 24, 1956 edition of *U.S. News & World Report* published an interview with Major William E. Mayer, United States army psychiatrist and one of the military's experts on brainwashing. Major Mayer confirmed for the first time in American history, nearly one-third of all American soldiers captured and imprisoned in Korea succumbed to brainwashing by the enemy:

... they became something called "progressives." By the Communist's own definition, this meant that a man was either a

Communist sympathizer or a collaborator – or
both – during his stay in a prison camp. (53)

When asked if military weakness was responsible,
the psychiatric expert answered, "No." He said "it is
something more than that. It goes deeper. The
behavior of many Americans in Korean prison
camps appears to raise serious questions about
American character, and about the education of
Americans." (54)

Major Mayer said in his opinion "the behavior of too
many of our soldiers in prison fell far short of the
historical American standards of honor, character,
loyalty, courage and personal integrity."

Mayer explained "this third that I am talking about
were not subjected to physical torture, according to
their own statements," *They surrendered to
brainwashing.*

He was very specific:

A returning prisoner often made reference to
the fact that he was given by the Communists a
very intensive education about America, a
Communist viewpoint of history which
evidently emphasized every possible defect in
our development and our attitudes, and the
soldier would confess that his own knowledge
of the American system – of our history, our
politics, our economics – was insufficient to
enable him to refute this Communist version,

even in his own mind. (55)

The Major defined brainwashing as "a calculated attempt to distort men's convictions and their principles... and to supply them with a mass of specific information." (56)

In short, brainwashing "is the eroding of the mind, the infiltrating of the spirit, and finally the paralyzing of the will. The men who withstand it are those whose minds are firm and clear and in possession of the truth." (57)

Dear Reader,

The objectives appearing in the final paragraph are the same objectives of *Yoga* – a highly misunderstood word from the Sanskrit language.

For more information on the communist indoctrination of children please read *Yoga and Going Green at School: The Truth Behind the Lies.*

My second book on this topic, *Understanding Yoga: Its Origin and Purpose* provides the necessary history; reveals the organizers and benefactors; and shares terrifying personal experiences from disciples of this ancient spiritual practice.

Thank you for reading Communism Brainwashing and the Birth of Public Schools.

May God bless you and yours,

Esther

Psalm 121

Recommended Reading

the deliberate dumbing down of america by
Charlotte Thomas Iserbyt

The SEICUS Circle by Claire Chambers

In the Presence of Our Enemies: A History of the
Malignant Effects in American Schools of the UN's
UNESCO and Its Transformation of American Society
From the Lips of Those Who Did it by Ellen McClay

Cloning of the American Mind: Eradicating Morality
Through Education by B.K. Eakman

The Leipzig Connection by Paolo Lionni

The Underground History of American Education by
John Taylor Gatto, New York State and New York
City Teacher of the Year

Dumbing Us Down: The Hidden Curriculum of
Compulsory Schooling by John Taylor Gatta

NEA: Trojan Horse in American Education by Samuel
L. Blumenfeld

The Transformation of the School by Lawrence A.
Cremin

The Turning of the Tides by Paul W. Shafer and John Howland Snow

None Dare Call it Education by John A. Stormer

References:

Chapter 1:

1. *NEA: Trojan Horse in American Education,* Samuel L. Blumenfeld, 1984, p 3
2. Ibid, pp 3-5
3. "The Bible in Schools," Dr. Benjamin rush, The American Tract Society, printed around 1830, reprinted 1995 by American Tract Society, Box 462008, Garland, TX, 75046
4. Ibid
5. *The New-England Primer*, Boston, Benjamin Harris, 1777, camera reproductions produced by Wallbuilder, Inc., 1991, TX wallbuilders.com
6. *NEA: Trojan Horse in American Education*, Samuel L. Blumenfeld, 1984, pp 7-8
7. Ibid, p 9
8. *Aim for the Children,* Daniel E. Johnson, 1997, pp 170-171
9. Ibid
10. *NEA: Trojan Horse in American Education,* Samuel L. Blumenfeld, 1984, p 10
11. Ibid, pp 10-11
12. Ibid, p 6
13. Ibid
14. Ibid, p 7
15. Ibid
16. Ibid, p 11
17. Ibid, pp 11-12
18. *Chronology of Education*, Dennis Laurence Cuddy, p 5

19. *NEA: Trojan Horse in American Education*,
    Samuel L. Blumenfeld, 1984, pp 11-12
20. Ibid, p 12
21. Ibid, p 13
22. Ibid
23. *Aim for the Children*, Daniel E. Johnson, 1997, p
24. Ibid, p 173
25. Underground History of American Education,
    John Taylor Gatto, 2001, p 171
26. *NEA: Trojan Horse in American Education*,
    Samuel L. Blumenfeld, 1984, p 17
27. Ibid, p 17
28. Ibid
29. Ibid, p 18
30. *Chronology of Education*, Dennis Laurence
    Cuddy, p 7
31. *Aim for the Children,* Daniel E. Johnson, 1997, p
    169
32. *Chronology of Education*, Dennis Laurence
    Cuddy, p 8

Chapter 2:

1. *the deliberate dumbing down of america,*
    Charlotte Thomson Iserbyt, 1999, p 2

2. *The Underground History of American Education,*
    John Taylor Gatto, NY State and NY City Teacher
    of the Year, 2000, p 270

3. Ibid

4. Ibid, p 271

5. *Dumbing Down Our Kids,* Charles J. Sykes, 1995,
    pp 201- 202

6. *The Underground History of American Education*,

(see above),   p 64

7.   Ibid, p 65

8.   *The Leipzig Connection: Basics in Education 1,* Paolo Lionni, 1993, p 1

9.   Ibid, p 9

10. Ibid, pp 8-9

11. Ibid, p 4

12. Ibid, p 2

13. Ibid, pp 8-9

14. *Brainwashing: The Story of Men Who Defied It,* Edward Hunter, 1956, pp 18-31

15. Ibid

16. *the deliberate dumbing down of america,* (see above), p 5

17. *Public Education Against America*, Marlin Maddoux, p 100

18. Ibid, p 98

19. *the deliberate dumbing down of america,* (see above), p 5

20. *The Leipzig Connection* (see above), pp 30-31

21. *The Transformation of the School,* Lawrence A. Cremin, 1961, pp 170-171

22. Ibid, p 172 and *the deliberate dumbing down of*

america (above), p 4

23. *The Underground History of American Education* (above), p 178

24. *NEA: Trojan Horse in American Education,* Samuel L. Blumenfeld, 1984, pp 82-83

25. *The Underground History of American Education* (see above), p 271

26. *NEA: Trojan Horse in American Education* (above) pp- 129-130

27. Ibid

28. Ibid

29. Ibid

30. *the deliberate dumbing down of america* (see above) pp 28-29

31. *The Underground History of American* Education, (see above) p 259

32. Ibid, p 273

33. *Science and Human Behavior*, B.F. Skinner, 1953, p 351

34. *the deliberate dumbing down of america* (above) p 43

35. Ibid, pp 44-45

36. *Bending the Twig*, Augustin G. Rudd,1957, pp 111-112

37. *NEA: Trojan Horse in Education*, (above) p 236

38. *the deliberate dumbing down of america* (see above) p 38

39. Ibid

40. Ibid, p 39

41. Ibid, p 49

42. Ibid, pp 49-50

43. Ibid

44. Ibid, p 109

45. Ibid, p 171

46. *Educating for the New World Order*, B.K. Eakman, 1991, p 170

47. the deliberate dumbing down of america, (see above), p 60

48. *Chronology of Education*, Dennis Laurence Cuddy, Ph.D., 1994, p 32

49. Ibid, pp 32- 33

50. Ibid, p 34

51. Ibid

52. Ibid, pp 100-101

53. *Brainwashing in the High Schools: An Examination of Eleven American History Textbooks*, E. Merrill Root, 1958, p 3

54. Ibid

55. Ibid, p 5

56. Ibid, p 4

57. Ibid

Proof Copy